BIBLE SKILLS, DRILLS, & THRILLS

ACTIVITY BOOK

A FUN-FILLED BIBLE SKILLS CURRICULUM FOR GRADES 4-6

Writers:
Pam Keith
Wanda King
Cindy Leach
June Mathews
Joanna Moore

LifeWay Press®
Nashville, Tennessee

GREEN CYCLE

ISBN: 0633194263
Item # 001244795

Dewey Decimal Classification Number: 220
Subject Heading: BIBLE-USE

Printed in the United States of America

Childhood Ministry Publishing
LifeWay Church Resources
One LifeWay Plaza
Nashville, Tennessee 37234-0172

We believe the Bible has God for its author; salvation for its end; and truth, without any mixture of error, for its matter and that all Scripture is totally true and trustworthy. The 2000 statement of *The Baptist Faith and Message* is our doctrinal guideline.

Table of Contents

Dear Parents,

We are happy to have your child be a part of Bible Skills, Drills, & Thrills.
Few things are more life changing than for a child to have the knowledge of God's Word and the ability to use his Bible effectively. In addition, he will have an opportunity to learn the books of the Bible, Bible book content, Bible history, Bible people, and life application.

Each week children will spend time learning Bible verses, the books of the Bible, and Key Passage titles and references. This year children will learn 25 verses and 10 Key Passages. You will find a poster showing the books of the Bible on page 77 and a Skills Check List on page 79. You can encourage your child by posting these in a prominent place.

We will use a variety of fun games and activities to teach the Bible skills and Bible material. Activities may include an active game, a quiet game, puzzles, a computer game, a music activity, a simple craft, or a writing activity. The group time will include a Bible story, prayer, verse memorization, practice using their Bibles, and life application of the story or verses. Children may choose between four hands-on application options: Bible Skills, Recreation, Crafts, or Service. All will relate to the Bible material.

Each of the 36 meetings will conclude with a special Family Bible Skills to Go Time. We hope that you will be able to attend this 5-10 minutes to learn more about what your child is learning.

You may wish to purchase a CD-ROM to use at home. This CD includes Scripture songs, books of the Bible song, and computer games to help your child develop Bible skills at home.

We are looking forward to having your child be a part of our group.

In Christ's Name

Psalm 119:105

Meeting 1

You Can Learn It!

Look at the pictures and see the many different ways you can display a Bible verse. Open your Bible to Genesis 1:1. Write the verse in each blank space. Each time you learn a verse you can write it on a card or a piece of paper and put it in a place to help you remember the verse.

The Bible, What's Different About It?

Can you think of things that make the Bible unique, different from other books? Using the letters of the word B I B L E write phrases or words that make the Bible unique.

Meeting 2

Who? Did What?

Genesis 1:1 says that In the beginning ...
Finish the verse by answering these questions.
Who? ____________________
Did what? ______________________________________

Read the verses and think about the days of creation. Draw a picture or write the words in the boxes showing what was created on that day.

Day 1 Genesis 1:1-3	Day 2 Genesis 1:6-8	Day 3 Genesis 1:9-13	Day 4 Genesis 1:14-19	Day 5 Genesis 1:20-23	Day 6 Genesis 1:24-31	Day 7 Genesis 2:1-3

No One Like Me

God created the world and everything in it. God made you unique. He made you in His image. Look at the words around the edges of the face. Which ones describe you? Draw them on the face or draw an arrow to the word that describes the area on the face.

Brown Hair
Black Hair
Green Eyes
Blue Eyes
Black Eyebrows
Red Eyebrows
Olive Skin
Freckled Skin

Red Hair
Blonde Hair
White Hair
Brown Eyes
Hazel Eyes
Blonde Eyebrows
Brown Eyebrows
Light Skin
Dark Skin

Meeting 3

Motions to Help You Learn

Find Exodus 20:12 in your Bible. Here are motions to match the memory verse. Learn the motion and write that portion of the verse under the motion box.

Attitudes and Commands

Match the wrong attitudes to one of the Ten Commandments.

Ten Commandments

1. There is to be nothing more important than God.
2. Don't make or use any object to worship that takes the place of God.
3. Don't misuse the name of God.
4. Set aside a day each week for worshiping God and resting from work.
5. Respect your parents.
6. Do not kill. Respect life.
7. Keep your marriage promises.
8. Do not take anything that belongs to someone else.
9. Do not lie. Always tell the truth.
10. Do not want anything that belongs to someone else.

Meeting 4

Match the phrases on the left to the correct word on the right.

More than one psalm is ...

Psalms is a book of ...

A particular song is a ...

Psalms

psalm

songs

Song of Praise

Use the dictionary provided to find the definition of *psalm*. Write it here:

Personal Praises

Highlight some of the words below that you use to describe God:

Write your own praise to God using words that you like to use. Each sentence has a different number of words. Follow the instructions along the side.

(5 words)

(4 words)

(3 words)

(2 words)

(1 word)

Meeting 5

Memory Pictures

Find Psalm 119:105 in your Bible. When you read that verse can you see word pictures?

Draw a simple picture for each of the words below. Then write the other words in the verse in between and around the pictures.

lamp

feet

light

path

How Can the Bible Help Me?

Look at the Bible below. Follow the paths to the different areas of your life. To the side write some ways the Bible can help you in those areas.

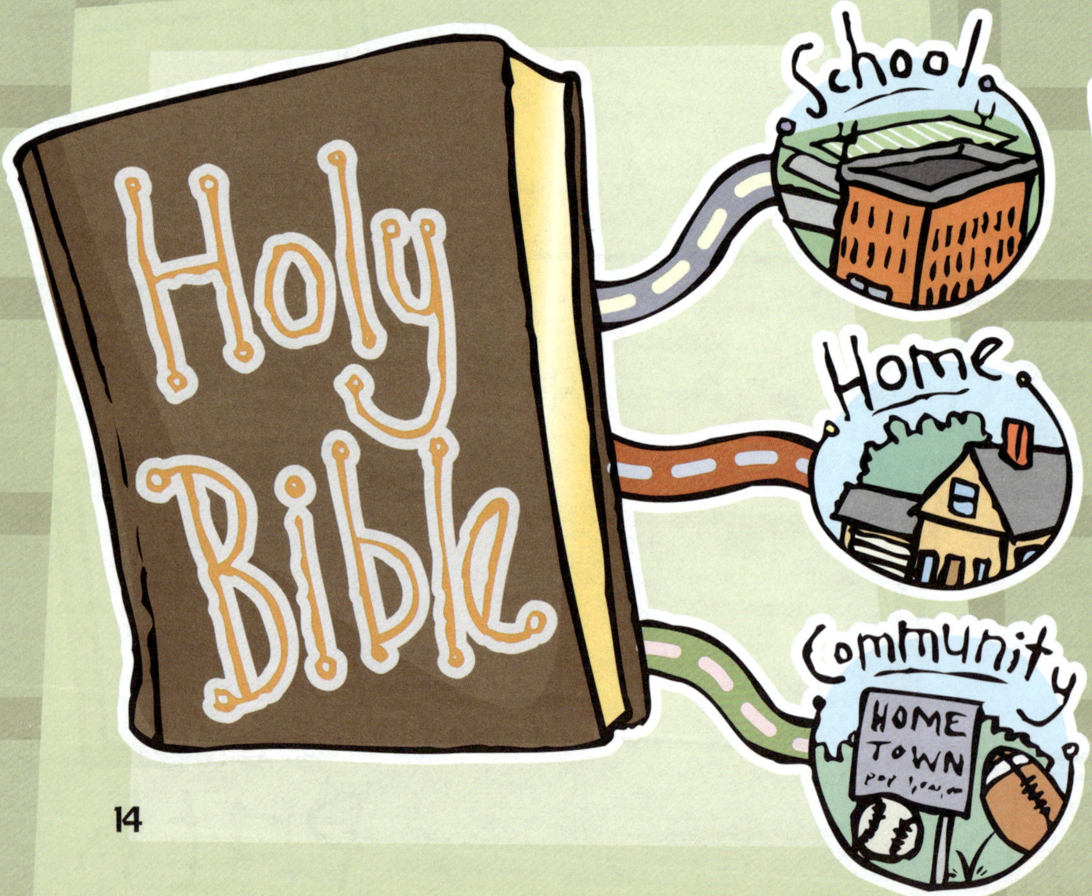

Meeting 6

There are verses in the Bible that say if you GET IT right, then you have GOT IT—God's promise.
Open your Bible to Proverbs 3:5-6.

Get it?

Write the first phrase of verse 5. Stop before the word *and*. Circle three words that you think are most important. How has God helped you when you trusted Him?

Write the first phrase of verse 6. If you want to obey this phrase, what can you do the next time you start to do something? Unscramble these letters to find out—RYPA

Got it!

Write the second phrase of verse 5. Have you ever trusted in your own self and gotten into a mess?

Write the last phrase of the memory verse. If you do all of the above what does God promise you?

Trusting God

THEN

God was faithful in Abram's life, and He is faithful in yours. In the circle draw something that God has done for you in the last five years:

NOW

What will you do for Him?
Look at next week. On each day, write one thing you will do for God. One day is completed for you.

Sun.	Mon.	Tues.	Wed.	Thurs.	Fri.	Sat.
Pray. Spend time with God.						

Meeting 7

What Does It Mean?

Read Proverbs 15:1. Look at the pictures. Write each phrase under the picture that it matches.

By the numbers list results you get when you react in those ways.

1. ______
2. ______
3. ______

1. ______
2. ______
3. ______

Situation Equation

Look at each situation. If you add a good attitude or bad attitude to the situation, what will be the results? Complete each equation:

Situation	+	= ?
Your little sister spilled nail polish on the bathroom floor.		
Your little sister spilled nail polish on the bathroom floor.		
Your parents let your brother choose the restaurant.		
Your parents let your brother choose the restaurant.		
Your parents couldn't afford to get you what you wanted for your birthday.		
Your parents couldn't afford to get you what you wanted for your birthday.		
You were picked for B team instead of A team.		
You were picked for B team instead of A team.		

Meeting 8

Unto Us a Child is Born

Find Isaiah 9:6 in your Bible. Fit four of the names of Jesus into the word grid. In the space below write other names that you call Jesus.

CHALLENGE Question!

In Luke 2, what name did the angel of the Lord use for Jesus?

He Promised!

Look for Bible verse references hidden in the temple. Write the reference beside the matching promise.

1. When you need help, God will be there for you.
2. When you are in trouble, God will help you.
3. If you want to get closer to God, He will come closer to you.
4. If you confess our wrong doings to God, He will forgive you.
5. If you love God, He loves you.
6. If you listen for God's direction, He will tell you the right thing to do.

Challenge!:

Luke 2:21-32: Who met Baby Jesus at the temple and knew the prophesy about him?______________________

Meeting 9

God Is . . .

Find and complete three words about God hidden in this broken puzzle. Then write Isaiah 40:8 in the space at the bottom.

Prayer Journal
Holy: to be set apart for religious use; sacred.
Eternal: lasts forever and ever
Unique: being one of a kind
Dear God, I praise you because you are
I praise you, God, because you are
I praise you, God, because you are
ERASER

Meeting 10

Depending on God

Find Nahum 1:7 in your Bible. Write in one slingshot the **fourth** word in the verse. In another slingshot, the **sixth** word. And in the final slingshot write the **third from the last** word found in the verse.

Find the words you have written on the slingshots in a concordance. Look for passages from the Book of Psalms. Choose verses that would make you feel better in a time of trouble. Discover verses that tell you how faithful and dependable God is.

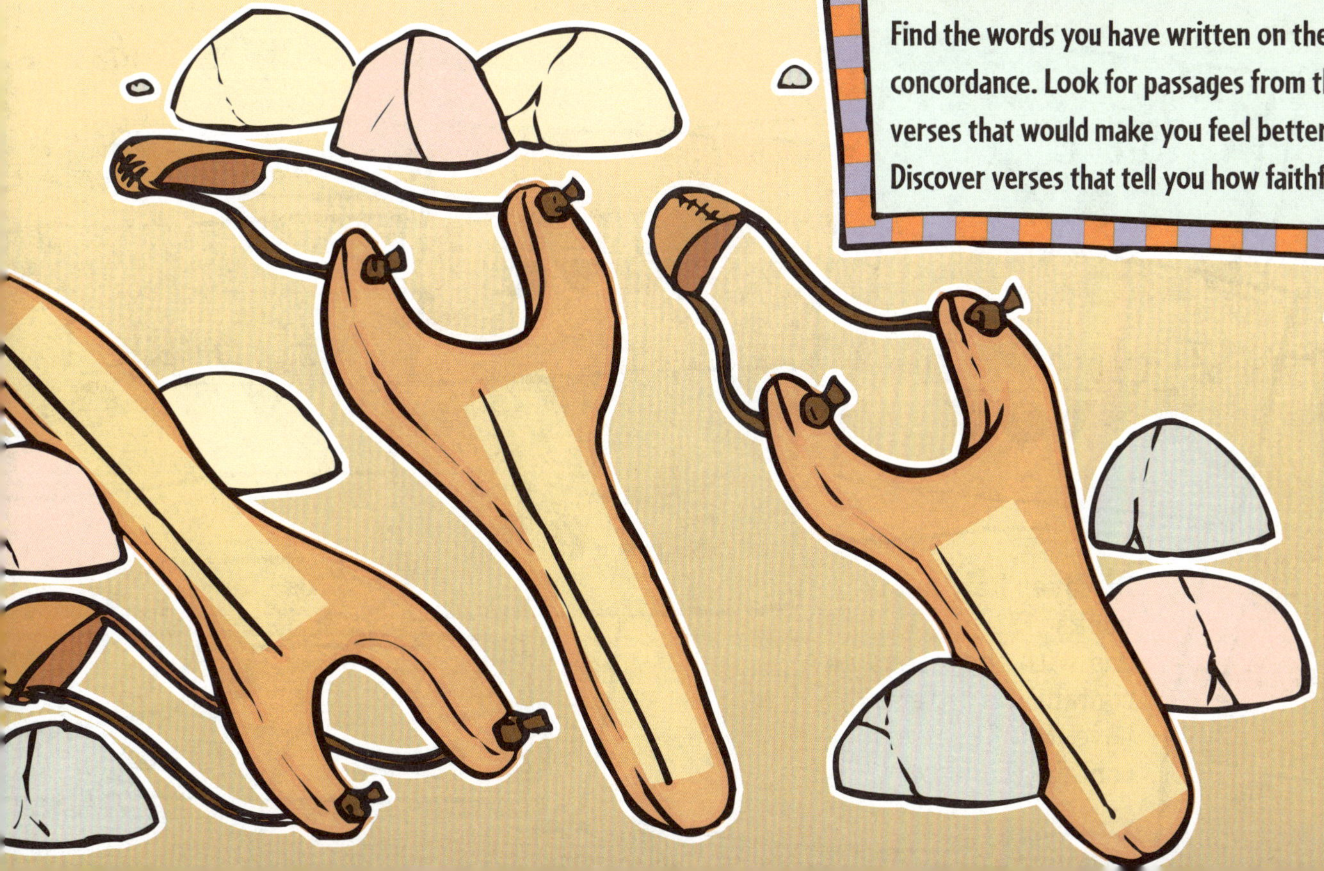

A **concordance** contains an alphabetical list of words that tells where you find those words in the Bible.

Decode the Minor Prophets

Use the code to decode the names of the Minor Prophets.

J_n_h
■▼

Z_ph_n_ _h
▲ ▼●▼

N_h_m
▼ ☼

M_l_ch_
▼▼ ●

H_s_ _
■▲▼

M_c_h
●▼

H_gg_ _
▼ ▼●

H_b_kk_k
▼▼ ☼

Z_ch_r_ _h
▲ ▼●▼

J_ _l
■▲

_b_d_ _h
■▼●▼

_m_s
▼■

Discover how many books . . .
end with the letters **ah**? ____
contain the letter **o**? ____
have **double** letters? ____
contain the letter **i**? ____

CODE
a: ▼ i: ● u: ☼
e: ▲ o: ■

Meeting 11

How Jesus Resisted Temptation

When Satan tempted Jesus in the desert, Jesus was able to resist the temptation Satan put before Him. Satan didn't use swords or shields. He tempted Jesus by quoting God's Word. The Bible says that the words of the Bible are like a sword. Use the clues below to find the verses of Old Testament Scripture that Jesus used as a weapon against Satan. Write the verse in the book below the clues.

1. The fifth book of Law
   Memory Verse Isaiah 40:___ : number of Old Testament books with a first and second (1 and 2)

   ________ ___:___

2. Book before the division of History begins
   Half the number of books of History : the number of books of Poetry + books of History - 1

   ________ ___:___

3. Book after the book of Numbers
   Number of Major Prophets + 1 : number of Minor Prophets + 1

   ________ ___:___

Challenge

First book of the Gospels

number of books in the division of the Gospels : number of books of Law + number of books of Poetry

Write this verse on the lines below.

____

____

____

____

Danger Ahead!

Find 1 Corinthians 10:13 in your Bible.
Is this....
good or bad news?

Fear

Impure

Lie

Disrespect

Cheat

Steal

Unkind

Meeting 12

Way to Live

Solve the first clue:

nd

5:16 in your Bible.

Find these words:

Write the complete verse:

People learn about God by watching the

The Code!

a b c d e f g h i j k l m n o p q r s t u v w x y z

The Love Law

Leviticus is one of the books of _____. Find Leviticus 19:18 in your Bible. This verse lays down the law to followers of God. Write what it says to you in your own words.

A neighbor is not just the person who lives beside you. Jesus taught that a neighbor includes everyone you meet. You should show mercy to everyone. Open your Bible to Luke 10:25-37. Read this story that Jesus told. What did Jesus tell the man to go and do?

Use a concordance to find other verses in the Bible that talk about loving your neighbor.

Meeting 13

Sermon Subjects

Match the Scripture reference to the picture and then write a summary of what the verses mean to you.

Matthew 5:38-39 and 7:1-5

Matthew 6:19-21

Matthew 6:5-13

STAINED GLASS JAR

materials needed:

newspaper (to protect your work area)

glass jar

tissue paper—several colors

scissors

small paintbrush

liquid starch or white glue and water

Choose a glass jar with a shape you like. Decide on the colors and design you want. Begin by tearing or cutting tissue paper into small shapes. Dip a small paintbrush into a mixture of liquid starch or half white glue and water. Brush the paper onto the jar. Press down any corners.

Forgiveness Champions

Meeting 14

Find Luke 6:37 in your Bible and write it here.

Forgiveness Champions are always on the lookout for people with judging, condemning, and grudge-holding attitudes! Write what the person might say after he remembers the actions of the other person.

Pledging Forgiveness

- List some things that members of your family do or say that bother you.
- List some things you do or say that bother your family members.

- Which is worse?
- You often think that what people do to you is worse. But how does the other person feel?
- What might happen if you were more understanding and patient with your family?

Talk about this as a family. Sign this pledge and put it up for all to be reminded this week.

We pledge to be more patient. We promise not to judge each other. We will be quick to forgive.

Signatures

Meeting 15

Knock on the Door

On each door is a Bible book. Write the book that comes before and after each book in the spaces provided.

Talking With God

In the spaces write things you might talk to God about when you are in the places pictured.

Meeting 16

Then and Now

Read John 3:1-21.

Talk to a friend about what Jesus said to Nicodemus?

How can you help a friend know how to be "born again"?

I can tell a friend how to be "born again" by using the **A B C**s.

A stands for __________ and the verse I can use is _______________.

B stands for __________ and the verse I can use is _______________.

C stands for __________ and the verse I can use is _______________.

Before and After...

Fill in the blanks with the names of the books of the Bible before and after the book named.

Gospel

Good news.
Christian message about the life and sacrificial death of Jesus Christ that brings salvation to all who believe.

______	Luke	______
______	Acts	______
______	Matthew	______
______	John	______
______	Mark	______

Meeting 17

Remember This...

How would you remember these important events? Match each event to the object that will help you remember the event.

- Your team winning the soccer tournament
- Participating in the science fair
- The details of your birth
- Your family vacation
- What Jesus did for you

CREATE A CODE TO CRACK

Use the code below to create a memory verse puzzle. Give your completed puzzle to a parent. See if they can crack the code and discover the verse.

A=E	I=O	U=A	H=S	M=Y	C=N	D=L	V=R	J=T
E=I	O=U	T=H	S=M	Y=C	N=D	L=V	R=J	

Meeting 18

Parable of the Sower

Jesus told a story about a farmer who sowed his seed on different types of soil. What did Jesus say each type of soil represented? Read Mark 4:1-20. Write your answers on each type of soil.

Sowing Key Passage Seed

Lay this page on the floor. Stand up and hold a sunflower seed about two feet over the page. Drop the seed onto the page. The seed should land on a Key Passage. Find that Key Passage in your Bible. State the Key Passage title and reference.

Meeting 19

Use the list of Bible books in your Bible to find a book that begins with each letter in the word *plan*. Write the name of the book next to the letter. How many chapters are in each of the books? Do you know the author? Use a Bible handbook if you need help.

Letter	Name of the book	Number of Chapters	Author
P			
L			
A			
N			

God can make THIS good?

Difficult things are happening to each of these kids. They have written a letter to tell God about it. Use your Bible to discover how God has a plan for each of these kids.

Dear God,
My mom and dad got divorced when I was little. Now, Mom is planning to get married again. I don't like that she is getting married, and we are fighting a lot. I'm so worried about all the things that are going to change. Please help!
Love, Jose

Dear God,
My schoolwork is getting really hard. I used to get straight As, but lately I am barely passing. I am so busy with soccer practice, piano lessons, and church activities. I feel stressed out all the time. My mom wants me to quit the soccer team. I don't know what to do. I need some help!
Love, Meg

Dear God,
My dad lost his job last yea Money is really tight. My shoes are awfully tight, but we don't have money for new ones. I heard Dad tell Mom that we might have to move out of our house if they can't make the payment. I'm afraid of what's going to happen.
Love, Andre

Dear Jose,
Read Matthew 6:25-27.
Love, God

Dear Meg,
Check out Proverbs 3:5-6.
Love, God

Dear Andre,
It's in Deuteronomy 31:8.
Love, God

Meeting 20

Start Your Engines

Match the correct key to start each car. And they're off!

Tell Your Story!

Paul's Story		My Story
Acts 22:1-5	Paul's Story ↔ My Story	Before I was a follower of Jesus
Acts 22:6-16	Paul's Story ↔ My Story	How I became a follower of Jesus
Acts 22:17-21	Paul's Story ↔ My Story	Now that I am a follower of Jesus

Meeting 21

Faithful Folks

Help these faithful folks find where their story is recorded in the Bible.

Gideon	Genesis 5:32–9:29
Noah	Judges 6–8
Joseph	Exodus
Moses	Genesis 12–18:15
Sarah	Genesis 37–50

Framing Faithful Friends

Draw a picture of someone you know who is faithful to God. Write on the lines how they show you their faith in God.

Meeting 22

Backward Alphabet

Backward Alphabet

ABCDEFGHIJKLMNOPQRSTUVWXYZ

My family is...

Families should be...

Seven Day Family Checklist

• My Family Scripture for the week is... ______________________

In the left-hand column of this chart, list some things you can do for family members in the coming week. Track your progress by checking off what you do each day.

Actions ↓	Mon.	Tues.	Wed.	Thurs.	Fri.	Sat.	Sun.
•							
•							
•							
•							
•							
•							
•							
•							
•							
•							
•							

Meeting 23 Force of Habit Survey

Put a check in the box that describes your life	Too Much	Too Little	Just Right	Not at all
I spend daily quiet time with God.				
I exercise regularly.				
I eat healthy foods.				
I limit my TV time and watch only wholesome shows.				
I play video games in limited quantities.				
I avoid inappropriate reading and Internet material.				
I avoid talking about others.				

Trail Mix

1 part plain dry cereal (rice, oat, or corn)

1 part candy-coated chocolate pieces

1 part dry-roasted peanuts

1 part raisins

Optional ingredients:

Dried fruit

Yogurt-covered nuts or raisins

Sunflower seed

Small pretzels or pretzel sticks

Place ingredients in large zip-lock bags, seal, and shake to mix.

Padre Punch

1 part ginger ale

1 part fruit punch

Pour into large bowl or pitcher. Serve with ice.

My Part for the Party is...

Meeting 24

Bible Story Roundup

Number the following statements 1 through 10 in order of occurrence.
If you need help, look in Genesis 37—45.

___ Joseph made himself known to his brothers.

___ Joseph's brothers sold him to some traveling salesmen.

___ Joseph's brothers were suddenly afraid of him.

___ Joseph's brothers returned to Egypt for food a second time, and at Joseph's request, brought their youngest brother, Benjamin.

___ Joseph and his brothers hugged and wept.

___ Joseph's brothers stole his beautiful coat and threw him into a pit.

___ Joseph told his brothers not to be upset because all that had happened was part of God's plan.

___ Joseph's father sent his brothers to Egypt for food the first time.

___ Joseph's father gave him a beautiful coat.

___ Joseph told his brother to go back home and get their father, families, and possessions and return to live with him in Egypt.

Range of the Home

Family Service Project Planning Sheet

Use this sheet to plan a family service project.

Proposed Project: ____

Proposed Date of Project: _______________________________________

Family Members Taking Part in Project: ____________________________

Project Leader: ____

What can we do to help?
Who will it benefit?
What abilities does our family bring to the project?
What materials, tools, and supplies will be needed?
How will our project be financed?
What are our transportation arrangements?

Additional preliminary tasks and assignments:

- ❑ Internet research on ______________________
  (Assigned to: ____________)
- ❑ Telephone calls to _______________________
  (Assigned to: ____________)
- ❑ Visits to _______________________________
  (Assigned to: ____________)
- ❑ Request information from ___________________
  (Assigned to: ____________)

Meeting 25

Determine which verse could best help you or a friend in each of the following fearful situations. Write its reference in the space provided. (Hint: There are no right or wrong answers. If you decide more than one verse applies or that a verse would help in more than one situation, write down more than one reference or use the reference more than one time.)

The Fear Factor!

Psalm 27:1,3
Psalm 91:4-6
Isaiah 41:13
John 14:27
Psalm 46:1
Proverbs 3:24
Isaiah 54:14
Hebrews 13:6

War or terrorism
Natural disasters
Serious illness or injury
(self, family member, or friend)
Death of a family member or friend
Family problems
Bullying or harassment
Failure in school
Rejection

My Church's Prayer Needs

Discuss with others some of the prayer needs you've heard about or noticed in your church.

Meeting 26

Who Said That?

Read the story of Jeremiah, Baruch, and the king in Jeremiah 36. Determine who might have said the following:

"But, Jeremiah, my hand is tired. Can we rest a minute?"
____

"Bring that scroll in here. I need something else to throw on the fire."
____

"Hey, guys, you're not going to believe this but there's a man standing near the entrance of the temple reading a scroll out loud." ____________________

"The king was so mad, it scared me half to death when he snatched the scroll out of my hand, started cutting it to pieces, and threw it on the fire. I'll never read for him again!" ____________________

"Jeremiah, let's write a book. I'll give you the words, you dictate them to Baruch and before you know it, we'll have a scroll." ____________________

"This could cause serious problems for you and Jeremiah. You two had better find a place to hide— and fast!" ____________________

"Hi, Baruch. I need somebody to write some things down for me. Will you help?" ____________________

"We're all going to be in big trouble if you burn that scroll, King. Please don't do it!" ____________________

Sending the Right Message

Read each unfinished statement and think about the messages you're sending to others. Complete each statement by writing the letter of the phrase that most truthfully describes your actions in the space provided.

Response key:

G = the way God would want me to.

O = OK, I guess. I could probably do better.

N = not like a very nice person at all.

How I welcome new kids at school and church is _____ .

The way I treat my sibling(s) is _____ .

The respect I show for parents, teachers, and others in authority is _____ .

The way I act around my closest friends is _____ .

My behavior at parties or other social gatherings is _____ .

The attention I pay to grandparents and other senior friends in my life is _____ .

My attitude toward waitresses, cashiers, and other people who serve me is _____ .

The thankfulness I give to God for everything He does for me is _____ .

Meeting 27

The People vs. Jesus

Answer the courtroom questions below with one of the words or phrases from the word list. For help, turn to John 19.

Word List

Chief priests
None
John
Crucifixion
Made Himself the Son of God (claiming to be a king)
Mary, the mother of Jesus, and Mary Magdalene
Guilty—He must die
The Pavement (in the temple complex)
A crowd of Jews
Pilate

1. Who was the judge in Jesus' case? (v. 1)
2. Who served as the jury? (v. 4)
3. What was the venue of the trial (where it took place)? (v. 13)
4. What evidence of a crime was given? (v. 7)
5. What were the charges against Jesus? (v. 12)
6. Who testified against Jesus? (v. 15)
7. What was the verdict? (v. 7)
8. What was the sentence? (v. 16)
9. Who were some of the eyewitnesses to the crucifixion? (v. 25)
10. Who documented (wrote down) what happened? (The book)

Words in Stone

Use words to describe the Bible and the space below to create a search-a-word puzzle. A few words have been listed for you, but you'll need to add more. Share the word search with family members.

GOOD BOOK

HOLY

INSPIRED

POETIC

TRUE

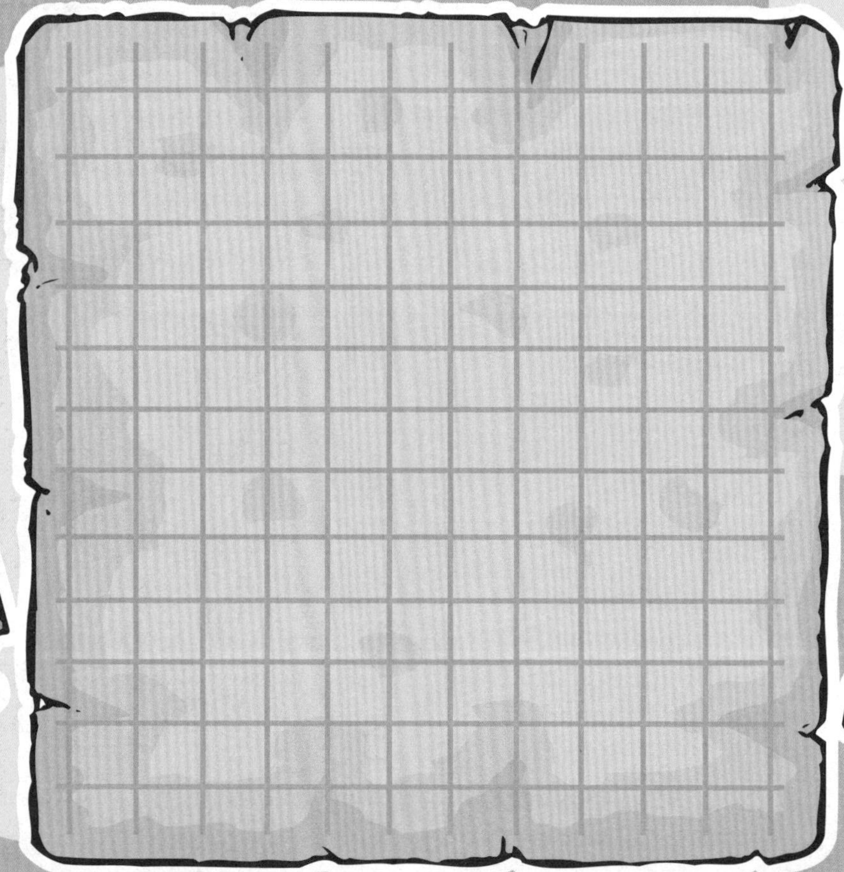

Meeting 28

Write a Litany

Follow each instruction. When you're finished you'll have a litany! If you have trouble thinking of a response sentence, ask a friend or leader for help.

Write a sentence of praise to God:

Write a response sentence:

Write a sentence telling why we should worship God:

Repeat the response sentence:

Write a sentence about something wonderful God created:

Repeat the response sentence:

Write a sentence about something wonderful God has done:

Repeat the response:

Write a sentence about how God helps us:

Repeat the response:

Write a sentence about giving thanks to God:

Repeat the response:

God's To-Do List

Refer to Genesis 1:1–2:3 to make a list of what He did each day of creation.

Day 1

Day 2

Day 3

Day 4

Day 5

Day 6

Day 7

Meeting 29

What?

Find and read Romans 5:8 and answer these questions:

Christ is another name for *Jesus*.

WHAT did God do?

WHAT did I do?

WHAT did Christ do?

Continue the Conversation:

How would you use the Bible passages and verses from today's meeting to continue the conversation in each of these case studies?

"I'm just going to give up. The harder I try to do the right things the worse I get. I can never be good enough for God to love me."

"Mia says that God is whatever you want Him to be. He is the ocean, the mountains, and the trees. That sounds strange to me. How can I really know God?"

"I got in trouble again at school today. I guess I was just born to be no good."

Meeting 30

An Eternal Equation

Use your Bible to complete this equation:

Following God's Plan

Unscramble the words in each sentence.
Label each file folder with the correct label.

Labels

Romans 10:13 **2 Corinthians 5:17**
Romans 10:9 **Romans 3:23**

mitAd that you are a ninser.

____

Evryenoe who calls on the name of the rdLo will be vedsa.

____

noCsefs and vebelei that Jesus is rdLo.

____

When a person aeptccs Jesus, there is a change in his havbeior.

____

Make an X in one of these boxes.

___ I have already asked Jesus to be my Savior.

___ I have been thinking about asking Jesus to be my Savior.

Meeting 31

Why Do I Need the Bible?

Find and read 2 Timothy 3:16 in your Bible.

What are four uses of the Scripture?

____

____

____

____

Why do you need the Bible?

The Walking Bible

Find and read 2 Corinthians 3:2 in your Bible.

Have you ever watched someone using sign language? Sign language is "talking" with your hands. God wants you to know that your life is a language that people read everyday. Some people who never read the written Bible watch the way you act. They listen to the words you say, and they decide what kind of person you are.

God wants you to be a walking Bible. He wants you to obey His Word so that people who see you will learn how great God is by reading you.

On each of the footprints write a way you can be a walking Bible.

Meeting 32

Ways to Honor My Parents

Obey them.

Be polite and respectful.

Be thoughtful.

Offer to help without being asked.

Do the right thing, even when they're not around.

Do my best at school.

Show appreciation for what they do for me.

Show love to them by my words and actions.

My Family Tree

Father's Side:

______ Great grandfather	______ Great grandfather
______ Great grandmother	______ Great grandmother
______ Grandfather	______ Grandmother

______ Father

Mother's Side:

______ Great grandfather	______ Great grandfather
______ Great grandmother	______ Great grandmother
______ Grandfather	______ Grandmother

______ Mother

______

______

______ children

Meeting 33

Book Search

Use the international Morse Code to write 2 Samuel 22:4 in code.

Scorecard for Self Scoring Book Drill:

Book:	Time 1	Time 2	Book:	Time 1	Time 2
Numbers			Job		
Mark			Isaiah		
Ephesians			Romans		
Hebrews			James		

- A ·–
- B –···
- C –·–·
- D –··
- E ·
- F ··–·
- G ––·
- H ····
- I ··
- J ·–––
- K –·–
- L ·–··
- M ––
- N –·
- O –––
- P ·––·
- Q ––·–
- R ·–·
- S ···
- T –
- U ··–
- V ···–
- W ·––
- X –··–
- Y –·––
- Z ––··

Hidden Clues

Find eight items hidden in this picture that are clues to events in David's life.

Meeting 34

Head Shots

Today's memory verse is a promise that God cares for you in all situations. Unscramble the names of these Bible people you have studied this year. How did God show that He cared for them?

TRUE OR FALSE?

The name of God is not mentioned in the Book of Esther.

Hopeless Hannah and Down-in-the-Dumps Dan

Explain to Hannah and Dan how God cares for them in each situation. Use the promise you learned in Romans 8:28.

Down-in-the-Dumps Dan

Hopeless Hannah

Meeting 35

Jonah's Journey

Track Jonah's journey by matching each sentence with the correct Scripture reference.

References: Jonah 3:5-10 Johah 4:1-11 Jonah 2:1-10 Jonah 1:1-3 Jonah 1:4-5 Jonah 1:13 Jonah 1:8-9 Jonah 3:1-4 Jonah 1:14-17

God said, "Go to Ninevah," but Jonah boarded a boat headed for Tarshish.

____

When God sent a storm, and the sailors were afraid.

____

Jonah told the sailors about God.

____

The sailors tried to row to shore.

____

After they threw Jonah overboard, the sea calmed, but Jonah was swallowed by a great fish.

____

Jonah prayed and the fish vomited him onto dry land.

____

Jonah went to Ninevah and preached God's message to the people.

____

The people of Ninevah repented, and God had compassion on them.

____

Jonah was angry, but God helped Jonah to understand His patience.

____

Lifelines

Jonah needed a lifeline when he was in the belly of the big fish. He prayed and God delivered him. Here are some boys and girls who need lifelines. Read each situation and each Scripture reference. On the life preserver, write the Scripture that will be a lifeline in that situation.

Cody realized he was a sinner when he was in the fourth grade. He is now a sixth grader. He has gone to VBS, Sunday School, and church camp every year. His teachers, leaders, and his pastor have invited him to accept Christ, but he has not.

____

Abbie made a commitment to have a daily quiet time. She tried it at night, but she was too tired. In the morning, she was too sleepy. She hasn't been reading her Bible for several weeks. She feels guilty. "God must be so angry with me," she wrote in her journal. "I've gone back on my word again and again."

____

Ever since Amanda's parents divorced, she can't sleep at night. She bites her nails and her stomach hurts every morning before school. The doctor s aid Amanda has anxiety attacks. "She worries about everything," her mom said.

____

Matt became a Christian when he was eight years old. Last year Matt made friends with a new boy from school. At a sleepover, Matt learned that his friend was a Hindu. After reading some books on that religion, Matt has decided that he wants to become a Hindu.

____

References

1 Peter 5:7	**2 Peter 3:9**
Lamentations 3:22-23	**Nehemiah 9:16-21**

Meeting 36

Family Celebration
Memory Verse Family Feud
Use these references to help you remember some of this year's memory verses.

2 Timothy 3:16

Revelation 4:11

1 John 1:9

2 Timothy 1:7

Exodus 20:12

Colossians 3:23

2 Samuel 22:4

Ephesians 4:32

Romans 8:28

1 Corinthians 4:2

FAMILY CELEBRATION SCORE SHEET

Place a sticker beside each activity as you complete it:

Thrill Ride Gameboard

Football Gameboard

Bible Computer Games

Saying the Books of the Bible

Memory Verse Family Feud

Awards Ceremony

Musical Bible Cards

Stackin' Game

Paper Plate Frisbee

Lazy Susan Game

Four Square

Bottled Water Give Away

Balloon Bop

Table Tennis Ball Pickup

Flyswatter and Balloon Relay

Medal Making

THE HOLY BIBLE

File Edit View Insert Format Font Tools Table Window Work Help Tues 12:52 PM

THE OLD TESTAMENT

LAW	HISTORY	POETRY	MAJOR PROPHETS	MINOR PROPHETS
Genesis	Joshua	Job	Isaiah	Hosea
Exodus	Judges	Psalms	Jeremiah	Joel
Leviticus	Ruth	Proverbs	Lamentations	Amos
Numbers	1 Samuel	Ecclesiastes	Ezekiel	Obadiah
Deuteronomy	2 Samuel	Song of Solomon (Songs)	Daniel	Jonah
	1 Kings			Micah
	2 Kings			Nahum
	1 Chronicles			Habakkuk
	2 Chronicles			Zephaniah
	Ezra			Haggai
	Nehemiah			Zechariah
	Esther			Malachi

THE NEW TESTAMENT

GOSPELS	HISTORY	PAUL'S LETTERS	GENERAL LETTERS	PROPHECY
Matthew	Acts	Romans	Hebrews	Revelation
Mark		1 Corinthians	James	
Luke		2 Corinthians	1 Peter	
John		Galatians	2 Peter	
		Ephesians	1 John	
		Philippians	2 John	
		Colossians	3 John	
		1 Thessalonians	Jude	
		2 Thessalonians		
		1 Timothy		
		2 Timothy		
		Titus		
		Philemon		

BIBLE SKILLS, DRILLS, & THRILLS

Skill Check List

❑ **Knows Books of the Bible**
❑ Old Testament
❑ Books of Law
❑ Books of History
❑ Books of Poetry
❑ Books of Major Prophets
❑ Books of Minor Prophets
❑ New Testament
❑ Books of Gospels
❑ Book of History
❑ Books of Paul's Letters
❑ Books of General Letters
❑ Book of Prophecy

❑ **Knows Bible Verses**
❑ 1. Genesis 1:1
❑ 2. Exodus 20:12
❑ 3. Psalm 118:24
❑ 4. Psalm 119:105
❑ 5. Proverbs 3:5-6
❑ 6. Proverbs 15:1
❑ 7. Isaiah 9:6
❑ 8. Isaiah 40:8
❑ 9. Nahum 1:7
❑ 10. Matthew 4:10
❑ 11. Matthew 5:16
❑ 12. Luke 6:37
❑ 13. Luke 11:9
❑ 14. John 3:16
❑ 15. John 15:12
❑ 16. Acts 16:31
❑ 17. Romans 8:28
❑ 18. Romans 12:1
❑ 19. 1 Corinthians 4:2
❑ 20. Ephesians 4:32
❑ 21. Colossians 3:23
❑ 22. 2 Timothy 1:7
❑ 23. 2 Timothy 3:16
❑ 24. 1 John 1:9
❑ 25. Revelation 4:11

❑ **Knows Bonus Verses**
❑ Romans 5:8
❑ Romans 10:9
❑ 2 Samuel 22:4
❑ Jonah 3:10

❑ **Knows Plan of Salvation References**
❑ Psalm 139:13-16; Romans 5:8; John 3:16; John 14:6
❑ Romans 3:23; Romans 10:9,13; 2 Corinthians 5:17

❑ **Knows Key Passages**
❑ The Ten Commandments: Exodus 20:3-17
❑ A Psalm of Praise: Psalm 100
❑ The Greatness of God: Isaiah 40
❑ The Temptation of Jesus: Matthew 4:1-11
❑ The Sermon on the Mount: Matthew 5–7
❑ Jesus and Nicodemus: John 3:1-21
❑ The First Lord's Supper: Luke 22:15-20
❑ The Parable of the Sower: Mark 4:1-20
❑ The Faith Chapter: Hebrews 11
❑ The Crucifixion: John 19

Name:______________________

BIBLE SKILLS, DRILLS, & THRILLS